The
Life Audit
Journal

ISBN 978-1-7972-2955-3

Manufactured in China.

MIX
Paper | Supporting
responsible forestry
FSC® C136333

Design by Wynne Au-Yeung.

10 9 8 7 6 5 4 3 2 1

Chronicle books and gifts are available at special quantity
discounts to corporations, professional associations, literacy
programs, and other organizations. For details and discount
information, please contact our premiums department at
corporatesales@chroniclebooks.com or at 1-800-759-0190.

Chronicle Books LLC
680 Second Street
San Francisco, California 94107
www.chroniclebooks.com

Find Your Purpose and Joy

The Life Audit

Journal

CHRONICLE BOOKS
SAN FRANCISCO

XIMENA VENGOECHEA

Contents

Introduction

Have you ever felt overwhelmed by your future, stuck in place and unsure of what to do next? Perhaps you feel as if you are living someone else's life or were meant to be doing something different, and you're wondering if it's too late to make a change. Maybe you have found yourself struggling with where to begin or have felt lost and uncertain about the path you have chosen. We've all compromised on our dreams at one point or another— or lost the thread on those dreams entirely. But you can reconnect with your early hopes and wishes. You can change how you live your life.

THE LIFE AUDIT

I've been there before too. Years ago, I was at a crossroads, amid a career change that included a promising cross-country move for a role I knew, deep down, wasn't right for me. The job was all numbers and spreadsheets when I preferred storytelling and imagery. I felt a constant tension between my ambitions and interests and the practical constraints and realities of this new role. Was this it? I wondered if I would ever be able to marry doing what I loved with making a living in any meaningful way. There was so much I wanted to do (projects to pursue, skills to acquire, experiences to have)—and even more I might want to do—and I didn't know where to start.

WHAt you LOVE   WHAt you GEt PAID to Do

THE hOLY GRAIL *
* WHAT'S yOURS?

It was during this time, when I was feeling both confused and overwhelmed, that the life audit—an exercise in self-reflection to help individuals uncover their values, desires, and life goals—was born.

LIFE
AUDIT.

(noun)

AN EXERCISE in SELF-REFLECTION that helps you CLEAR the COBWEBS of noisy, EXTERNAL goALs and CURRENT distRACTions, and REVISIT or UNCOVER the REAL themes and CORE VALUES that DRIVE and INSPIRE you. ALSO KNOWN AS SPRING-CLEANING for the SOUL.

The life audit is a system I developed to help me figure it all out. It is a step-by-step process for surfacing deep-seated desires and making sense of them. It employs best practices from my training in user research, a field that helps us understand the underlying needs, motivations, feelings, behaviors, and perceptions that stem from deep within us. Research tricks of the trade like brainstorming, mapping data, and pattern analysis had helped me synthesize large amounts of data into insights before. Why not take this same process of alchemy—a step-by-step approach that is practical yet feels magical—and apply it to my own life?

The life audit gave me clarity then, and at every major crossroads since. My life audits have shown me where change was needed and where I already had momentum in making my dreams come true. They have shown me whether my daily life was pushing me toward or away from my dreams, values, and purpose. While I'd initially thought of the life audit as a simple prioritization tool that would help me figure out what to do next, it took me deeper than I'd imagined.

This simple activity set my life in motion in ways I could not have anticipated; it is in large part the reason for my writing career, and why I've written three books (and counting), along with the journal you're holding right here. The life audit was the spark, the beginning of it all.

Years later, I return to the practice whenever I am feeling lost and unmoored or brimming with ideas I've yet to organize. It has helped me to navigate—or led me to—cross-country moves, career changes, relationship changes, and other life milestones. I return to it annually to check in with myself on what goals still feel relevant and what new dreams and desires have cropped up.

Although I first developed the life audit for myself, it has brought clarity and direction to many others since then. From developing their intuition or setting more boundaries, to getting divorced, changing careers, or prioritizing more family time, the life audit has helped many to discover new hidden desires, revisit long-standing wishes or goals, and pursue their hopes and dreams with clarity and conviction in heart and mind. May it do so for you too.

HOW TO USE THIS JOURNAL

The Life Audit Journal is an invitation to rediscover your values, passions, and dreams. It is a safe space for dreaming big, a kick start for dreams previously on hold, and an honest gut check for honoring our values and desires every day. It is a way to prioritize your goals and turn personal insights into action. It is a place to safeguard your thoughts, to return to your self-reflections, to measure your progress as often as you'd like. It is a tool that makes it simple to find personal clarity and architect the life you want.

This journal answers essential questions like

- What are my goals?

- What are my values?

- Am I spending my time aligned with these goals and values?

- What's getting in my way?

- How nourishing are my relationships?

- Do I have the right people in my corner to realize my goals, aspirations, and intentions?

- What should I do next?

- What is a priority now versus later?

- What resources do I need to make progress?

In *The Life Audit Journal*, you'll find prompts to help you self-reflect and uncover the deepest desires, goals, wishes, and values within you. You'll also find exercises to help you understand your wishes, determine how to prioritize them, and solidify when and how to act on them. In addition, you'll find handy ribbon markers to keep track of your wishes as you begin to make meaning of them. Use this journal as a tool for understanding yourself and your goals more deeply. You'll find meaningful prompts for self-assessment, self-discovery, and self-actualization. At the end of the journal, you'll also find a place to capture any additional notes, observations, and questions you want to return to in more detail later.

You can answer these questions all in one go, during a weekend marathon session or a long flight. Or you can dive deep over the course of a few months, when you are faced with a big life change and seeking more clarity. You might even go bit by bit, day by day to anchor your daily activities and keep your personal core values in check. There is no wrong way to journal your way through your life audit: Simply go at your own pace and find what works best for you.

In these pages you'll explore four themes: where you are today, what you want, what it means, and what you can do about it. With these personal insights, you can begin to make changes—some big, some small—and live the life you want.

This journal is a companion to *The Life Audit* book, which outlines the steps to conducting your own life audit in more detail, but you can also use this journal on its own. If you enjoy this journal, you might like the book as well. It is the perfect complement to your *Life Audit Journal* on your journey of self-discovery—a way to go even deeper into what you've learned about yourself.

THE BEST TIME FOR A LIFE AUDIT

When should you conduct your life audit? Many people find this exercise to be especially useful during moments of transition and uncertainty. When we face a personal crossroads, such as a career change, geographic move, birthday, graduation, retirement, new parenthood, or more, clarity and direction can be an encouraging balm. Others schedule annual New Year's life audit sessions; by the end of the year, most of us are naturally in an introspective mindset. It's a great time to reflect on audits past and appreciate how far we've come.

Why WE AuDit

WE ARE at a CROSSROADS

WE aRE READy for a ChANgE

WE ARE OVERWhELMED By ouR AMBITIONS

WE ARE UNSURE of WhAt WE WANt

WE ARE SEEKING iNSPIRAtioN

WE WANT TO FEEL COMPLETE

WE WANT A LIFE BEyoND ouR JoBS

WE WANT TO GET TO KNOW OURSELVES

WE ARE SEEKiNG FoCuS

Sometimes it is obvious to us why we are called to dig deeper, but other times it is hidden. Ultimately, you should conduct your life audit whenever the spirit moves you. When you're seeking clarity or wanting to reconnect with yourself. When you're in need of direction and encouragement. When you're ready to dig deep into what it is you want from this life and what's getting in your way. You needn't wait for a special date or occasion to think more deeply about your life. When you can find the time, space, and mental energy to answer meaningful questions about your life, the moment is right.

Now that you've arrived, let's get started.

Happy life auditing,

XIMENA

PART 1

Starting Off

WHERE DO THINGS STAND?

How am I doing?
Fill in the blanks and tell your story.

HOW I FEEL ABOUt my LiFE TODAy:

THE PARts I LOVE ARE:

ONE THING I WISH I COULD CHANGE:

I'M AFRAID to ADMIT thAt whAt I REALLY WANT IS TO:

OVERALL, I FEEL MY LIFE is:

I AM HEADING in the

☐ RIGHT
☐ WRONG

diRECTION

What's working well?
List five things bringing you satisfaction, joy, or ease in your life.

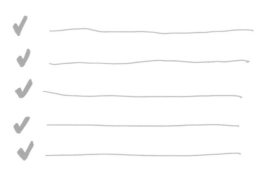

What could be better?
List five things that give you grief, stress, or worry in your life.

HOW am I DOING?

HERE am I GOING?

WHAT'S IMPORTANT NOW THAT WASN'T BEFORE?

I HAVE LOST MY BEARINGS. I AM LOOKING FOR MY TRUE NORTH

Why am I here?

What's bringing you to this life audit? Share your story.

How do I typically spend my time?

Jot down the five to ten activities you spend the most time on, on average, to see your "pointless to purposeful ratio"—or how much time you spend on things that are meaningful and aligned with your values and goals, versus everything else.

1. _____

2. _____

3. _____

4. _____

5. _____

6. _____

7. _____

8. _____

9. _____

10. _____

Map your list of top activities to the circles below. Label each circle according to how much time you dedicate to each activity. Use big circles to represent how you spend the bulk of your time and small circles to show where you spend only a little of your time. Add more circles as you see fit.

WHERE DOES YOUR TIME GO?

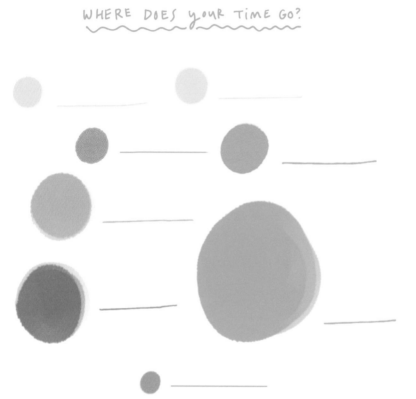

WHERE DOES THE TIME GO?

PERCEPTION	REALITY
WORK	MEMES
SLEEP	DOOM-SCROLLING
CHORES	LIST MAKING
SOCIALIZING	TEXTING

Are you happy with how you spend your time?
Be honest in your response.

In an ideal world, what changes would you make to how you spend your time?

Fill in the blanks to show how you would ideally spend your time. Notice any gaps between how you'd ideally spend your time and how you actually spend your time.

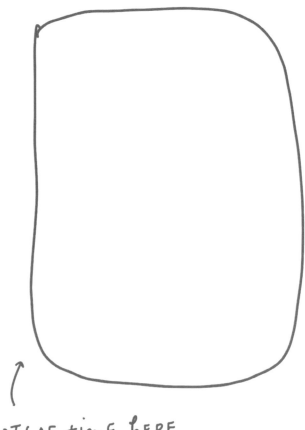

LOTS OF tiME hERE

JUST A
SMIDGE
HERE

29

Who gets my time?

The law of averages suggests that our success is determined by the five people with whom we spend the most time. List the top five people with whom you spend time on a regular basis. These are people who get lots of headspace and company from you. Be specific.

1. _____

2. _____

3. _____

4. _____

5. _____

THE COMPANY WE KEEP

THE COMPANY WE SEEK

NEIGHBORS
COLLEAGUES
ROOMMATES
FAMILY
PARTNERS

ADVISORS
MENTORS
FRIENDS
CONFIDANTS
ROLE MODELS
SUPPORTERS

good
eggs

Are you in good company?

Looking at your list, are you happy about whom you spend your time with? Do you have the right people in your corner? Write down your overall thoughts in response to your list.

What do they bring to the table?

As you reflect on the company you keep, think about what they bring to your relationship and what might be missing. Check all that apply on the following list:

DOES the COMPANY I KEEP...

☐ INSPIRE ME

☐ TEACH ME

☐ SUPPORT ME

☐ MENTOR ME

☐ CHEER ME ON

☐ LIFT ME UP

What changes do you want to make?

Answer the following questions to complete the chart. Who would you like to see more of? Less of? Whose company is just right? Who is not on this list but should be? Add their names to this chart.

⊕ MORE OF	⊖ LESS OF

✓ JUST RIGHT	⊙ MISSING

PART 2

Dreaming Big

Make a list of every wish, goal, or desire you have for yourself in this life.

Give yourself an hour to dream and aim for a hundred wishes. No wish, goal, or desire is too big or too small. You might include everything from a desire to be more patient to an intention to get a promotion, to call home more, or to learn how to make a podcast. A wish can come in the form of a concrete goal, or it can be as amorphous as a feeling you want more of in your life (for example, to experience more joy or play). The number is just a guidepost: Don't feel pressured to reach or limit yourself to one hundred. List your wishes out on the following pages, and use a ribbon marker to keep your place: You will reference this list throughout the journal.

1. _____

2. _____

3. _____

4. _____

5. _____

6. _____

7. _____

8. _____

9. _____

10. _____

11. _____

12. _____

13. _____

14. _____

15. _____

16. _____

17. _____

THERE IS SO MUCH MORE THAT I CAN DO IN THIS WORLD

18.

19.

20.

21.

22.

23.

24.

25.

26.

27.

28.

29.

30.

31.

32.

33.

34.

35.

36.

37.

38.

39.

40.

41.

42.

43.

44.

45.

46.

47.

48.

49.

50.

51.

52. _____

53. _____

54. _____

55. _____

56. _____

57. _____

58. _____

59. _____

60. _____

61. _____

62. _____

63. _____

64. _____

65. _____

66. _____

67. _____

68. _____

69. _____

70. _____

71. _____

72. _____

73. _____

74. _____

75. _____

76. _____

77. _____

78. _____

79. _____

80. _____

81. _____

82. _____

83. _____

84. _____

85. _____

86.

87.

88.

89.

90.

91.

92.

93.

94.

95.

96.

97.

98.

99.

100.

Are you being honest with yourself?

Looking at your list, cross off any wishes that feel like something you *should* do more than *want* to do. Leave only what you really, truly wish to do. If you don't have any "shoulds" on your list, this is a sign that you are being true to yourself.

"SHOULD" WISHES	TRUE WISHES
HAVE a KID	WORK with KIDS
BECOME a LAWYER	BECOME an ARTIST
TRAVEL	NEST
MAKE MY PARENTS HAPPY	MAKE MYSELF HAPPY
GET PROMOTED	SWITCH CAREERS
STUDY MORE	PLAY MORE

What do you notice about your "shoulds"?

What patterns do you see? For example, perhaps your "shoulds" are all about family or work.

Where do these beliefs about what you "should" be doing with your life come from?
Think about the people, culture, and organizations in your life influencing your thinking.

What themes do you see in your wishes?

Examples of themes you may encounter are finances, beliefs, values, or hobbies. (Note that there are many others, and none of these are required. See the following illustration for inspiration.) You may notice that some themes overlap with others. If a wish fits in more than one theme, choose the theme that feels most relevant to you. Make a list of your themes below.

THEMES to help you GET STARTED

LEISURE
time

COMMUNITY

FAMILY

HEALTH

SPIRITUALITY

CREATIVE
PURSUITS

ADVENTURE

RELATIONSHIPS

CAREER

Which themes are most present for you?
Least present?

Count the number of wishes in each group or theme. Tally them below.

THEME

WISHES PER THEME

_____   _____

_____   _____

_____   _____

_____   _____

_____   _____

_____   _____

_____   _____

_____   _____

_____   _____

_____   _____

_____   _____

Overall, what do you see?

Using the numbers you tallied, fill out this bar chart to see
where your dreams net out. Label each theme along the x-axis,
then fill in the bar chart along the y-axis with the number of
wishes in each theme. Notice the top five themes.

A LIFE'S WORTH of WISHES,

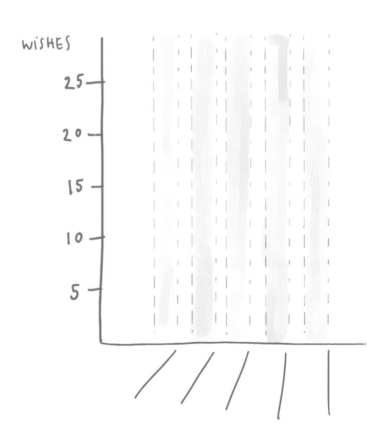

SORTED BY tYPE

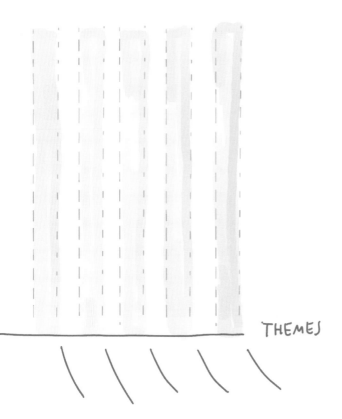

THEMES

WISH	CORE VALUE
TO SLOW DOWN	PEACE, CALM, PATIENCE, REST
TO BE KIND	KINDNESS, COMPASSION
TO BE MORE GENEROUS	EMPATHY, GENEROSITY
TO BE A GOOD FRIEND	COMMUNITY, LOYALTY
TO BE THERE for my FAMILY	DUTY, FAMILY, TRADITION
TO SHARE my LEARNINGS	TEACHING, MENTORSHIP, COACHING
TO BE MORE VULNERABLE	INTIMACY, SELF-AWARENESS
TO BE my OWN ADVOCATE	SELF-RESPECT, SELF-WORTH
TO TRUST my INTUITION	SELF-CONFIDENCE, FAITH, INNER WISDOM

Which wishes represent your core values?

Your core values reflect beliefs and intentions about what it means to live a good life and be a good person. (For example, a wish to call home more often might be rooted in a belief that we owe our families our time and attention.) Pull out the wishes on your list that are rooted in personal core values and list them in the chart on the following page.

What deeper value do these wishes point to?

See if you can uncover what core value your wishes are rooted in. Make a list of their corresponding core value on the right.

WISH	CORE VALUE

What do you notice about your core values?

Do you feel surprised or validated by how they appear in your life audit? Share your observations below.

I WANT TO

rust my INTUITION

BE A GOOD FRIEND

BE GENEROUS

LOW DOWN

In an ideal world, when would you pursue these dreams?

Returning to your list of wishes bookmarked on pages 39–45, mark when you hope to see them through, using the following symbols:

Mark a heart next to wishes you want to see through every day. These are often core values, like "to be patient."

Next, draw an arrow for wishes you might pursue in the near term, in the next six to twelve months. For example, publishing your first blog post, getting a personal trainer, and getting off your family cell plan could all be *soon* goals.

Finally, draw a star next to long-term goals and milestones, like buying a house, falling in love, or hitting the bestseller list.

What do you notice about your wishes now?

Don't worry about whether your timeline feels feasible or not just yet. Simply notice which wishes you feel ready to invest in now versus later.

I WANT TO DO THE THINGS I'VE ALWAYS SAID I WANTED TO DO

STRETCHING
BREAK

Now is a great time to stretch
your body, roll out your neck,
and shake your hands out before
moving to the next section.

PART 3

Understanding Myself

WHAT

HAVE

I

LEARNED?

What can my wishes tell me about myself?

Review your list of wishes bookmarked on pages 39–45.
What are your wishes revealing to you? Jot down your first
impressions here, then fill in the blanks on the opposite page.

Something that SuRPRISEd ME:

Something that FELt
NEW to ME:

Something that FELt tRUE
to ME:

What can my wishes tell me about my regrets?

Notice whether feelings of regret, self-criticism, or longing come up as you look at your list. These may reflect missed opportunities, past mistakes, self-limiting beliefs, others' expectations, or circumstances beyond your control. Pay attention to areas where these feelings arise. Jot down your impressions below, then fill in the blanks on the opposite page.

Something I REGRET NOT PRIORITIZING SOONER:

Something I BLAME MYSELF FOR OR am SELF-CRITICAL ABout:

A STORY OR SELF-LIMITING BELIEF I WANT to LET go of:

What can my wishes tell me about my desires?

Our wishes can reveal our innermost desires and deeply held beliefs. Some of these will be familiar to us, but some may be surprising. We may even discover desires we've never said aloud.

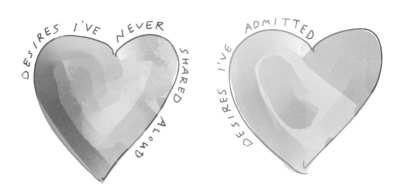

Use the space on the following page to explore the kinds of desires that come up for you in your audit.

SECRET DESIRES

REPEAT DESIRES

THAT'S SO "ME"
DESIRES

OTHER OBSERVATIONS

I AM UNEARTHING MY TRUE DESIRES

What can my wishes tell me about my ambitions?

For example, perhaps you have discovered a desire to make a difference in your community or unearthed a secret wish to be well-liked or even famous. List three ambitions you've discovered.

1. _____

_____

2. _____

_____

3. _____

_____

What can my wishes tell me about my values?

List three values you've discovered.

1. _____

2. _____

3. _____

WHAt can my WISHES tELL ME

MY MINDSET

MY PRIORITIES

MY COMPANY

ABOUT HOW I LIVE MY LIFE TODAY?

MY BELIEFS

Anything ELSE

MY TIME

What did I learn about myself through my wishes overall?

Do you feel surprised or validated by how your values, beliefs, priorities, and ambitions surfaced in your life audit? Share your observations below.

You may find that some areas of your life are flourishing, while others could use some more attention. This is normal. Knowing where things stand can help us chart a path forward.

WHAT NEEDS ATTENTION?

WHAT is WELL TENDED?

What is well tended to?

List three areas of your life that are in good shape. These may be values you regularly uphold, dreams you already have in motion, or important parts of your life that did not show up in your life audit as wishes because you are already tending to them.

1. _____

   _____

   _____

2. _____

   _____

   _____

3. _____

   _____

   _____

How have I tended to these in the past?

Think about the personal qualities, skills, talents, support, or strategies that have helped you uphold these values and make progress in the past.

PERSONAL QUALITIES

SKILLS + TALENTS

EXTERNAL SUPPORT

STRATEGIES + PHILOSOPHIES

Are there any areas that need attention?

List your top three. These may be areas you have inadvertently deprioritized or where you have let your values lapse.

1. _____

_____

_____

2. _____

_____

_____

3. _____

_____

_____

How or why have I neglected these areas?

Think about what might have been missing (skills, talents, support, strategies, or other resources) or getting in your way (emotions, competing priorities, extenuating circumstances, etc.).

◇ MISSING PIECES ⟨₃

△ ROADBLOCKS △

_____   _____
_____   _____
_____   _____
_____   _____
_____   _____
_____   _____
_____   _____
_____   _____

What do my wishes tell me about my feelings and emotions?

Think about which emotions your wishes are most closely connected to.

WISH	EMOTION or NEED
TAKE MORE URBAN ADVENTURES	FUN, JOY, PLAY
LEARN REIKI and MASSAGE	PEACE, CALM
WORK ON my MARRIAGE	LOVE, LONELINESS
TRY TAROT	CLARITY, TRUTH, WISDOM
MAKE MORE MONEY	PRIDE, JOY

WARM
EMOTIONS
(PASSION,
EXCITEMENT,
CONTENTMENT)

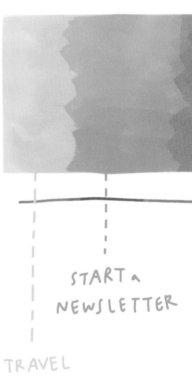

START a
NEWSLETTER

TRAVEL
ABROAD

BY EMOTION

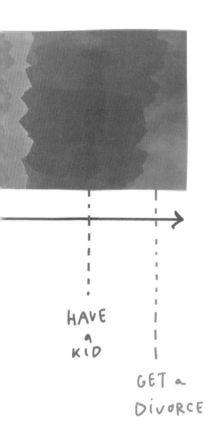

COOL
EMOTIONS
(FEAR, ANGER,
INSECURITY)

HAVE
a
KID

GET a
DIVORCE

Am I surprised by this?

Think about where your emotions are getting in the way of pursuing your dreams, and where they may be helping your cause.

Which wishes feel daunting or scary?
List them out.

Why might this be?
Check all that apply:

WHAT MAKES THESE WISHES FEEL DAUNTING?

☐   I am SCARED to TRY SOMETHING NEW

☐   I FEEL OVERWHELMED BY THE SIZE of THESE GOALS

☐   I FEEL UNINSPIRED BY THESE GOALS

☐   SOMETHING ELSE . . . !

Say more about what might be causing you to feel this way.

WHAT AM I AFRAID OF?

How have I overcome similar fears in the past?

Which wishes feel inviting or exciting?
List them out.

Why might this be?
Check all that apply:

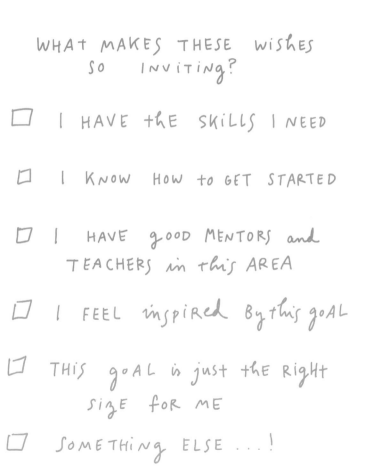

WHAT MAKES THESE WISHES
SO INVITING?

☐ I HAVE the SKILLS I NEED

☐ I KNOW HOW to GET STARTED

☐ I HAVE good MENTORS and
TEACHERS in this AREA

☐ I FEEL inspired By this goAL

☐ THIS goAL is just the RIGHT
SIZE FOR ME

☐ SOMETHING ELSE . . . !

Say more about what might be causing you to feel this way.

Your life audit can offer a new perspective on your hopes and dreams.

BEFORE and AFTER

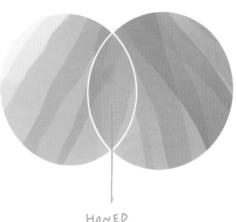

WHAT I
THOUGHT
I WANTED

WHAT
I KNOW
I WANT
NOW

HONED
INTUITION

What's changed in the process of conducting my life audit?

Fill in the blanks.

I THOUGHT I WANTED THIS

_____

_____

_____

_____

_____

_____

_____

_____

_____

_____

_____

_____

I ACTUALLY WANT THAT 🌙⭐

_____

_____

_____

_____

_____

_____

_____

_____

_____

_____

_____

_____

What do my wishes say about me?
Use the fill in the blanks below as thought starters.

I am a person who . . .

cares a lot about _____

_____

is preoccupied by _____

_____

is seeking _____

_____

is happiest when _____

_____

feels most fulfilled by _____

_____

believes in _____

_____

is motivated by _____

_____

What are three big takeaways from my life audit?

THREE   BIG   TAKEAWAYS

1

2   3

PART 4

Taking Action

WHAT CHANGES CAN I MAKE?

To best navigate our many wishes and personal insights, we need to prioritize and choose where to start.

Here are a few ways you might consider prioritizing your wishes:

By emotion: Choose what makes you scared, excited, joyful, or a mix.

Using rational thinking: Start with what you know you can achieve and consider which resources you have in place or how reaching one goal will help you reach others.

By complexity: Choose many small, straightforward goals you know you can easily achieve, or select only a handful of stretch goals to work toward.

By resources: Consider how "expensive" a goal will be to fulfill (in time, money, equipment, or other resources) or estimate how much time will be needed to complete it (because of its complexity or scope), versus which goals have little start-up cost.

By the numbers: Use the frequency of how often a goal, value, or wish appears in your life audit and which themes are most numerous as your guides and go with your biggest piles first.

By intuition: Go with your gut and trust it's telling you where to start for a reason.

HEART PRIORITIES ♥ ◉ HEAD PRIORITIES ◉

FALL in LOVE

PAY off my LOANS

LIVE a good LIFE

What does my heart want?

What does my head want?

What would bring me the most joy in life?

WHAT WOULD BRING ME JOY IN LIFE?

Which wishes make me feel most aligned with my values?

List them here.

_____

_____

_____

_____

_____

_____

_____

_____

_____

_____

_____

_____

_____

_____

What is more than I can take on at this moment?

Think about which wishes are too complicated to pursue right now, either because they are time or resource intensive, require acquiring a new skill set, or are emotionally taxing beyond what you are capable of right now.

Which wishes feel like obligations?

Some wishes may be obligations in disguise. If it feels like a chore or responsibility, jot it down here.

Which wishes feel like true desires?

What feels doable to pursue right now?

Of all the wishes on my list, where do I want
to start?
Choose up to five wishes you will pursue this year. Add them
to the following page.

✧ my top five wishes ✧

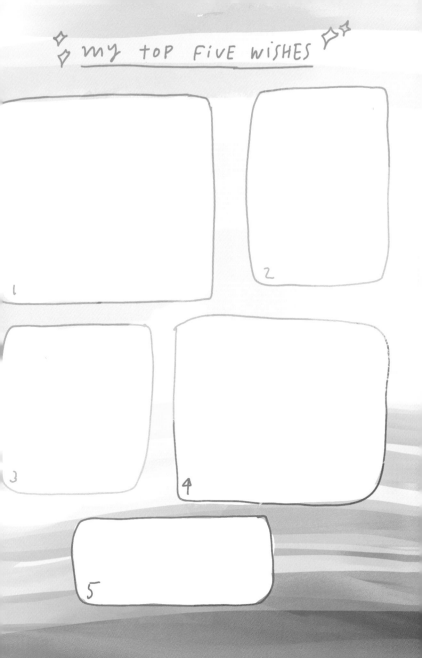

1

2

3

4

5

What obstacles might get in my way?

Get ahead of potential hurdles by identifying them up front. Examples of hurdles you might face in pursuit of your dreams include responsibilities, feelings and emotions, resources, or skills. Consider what is standing in your way and jot them down on the following page. Be specific.

WHAT'S STANDING IN YOUR WAY?

SELf-Limiting BELiefs

PARENTAL PRESSURE

SOCiETAL EXPECTATIONS

Ø my top five HURDLES Ø

1

2

3

4

5

How have I managed these kinds of obstacles in the past?

Jot down five tools, resources, strategies, skills, or talents that have helped you surmount these kinds of hurdles before. If you are having trouble recalling how you have surmounted hurdles in the past, think about the tools that could be most useful moving forward.

my top FivE TooLs

1

2

3

4

5

Make an action plan for your dreams, starting with your top five priorities.

your Life Audit

your Action Plan

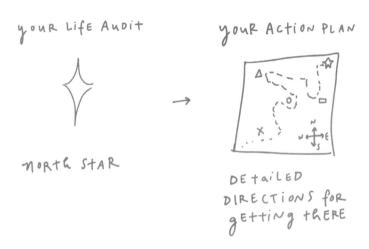

NORTH STAR

DEtaiLED DIRECTioNS foR getting thERE

Return to the top five wishes you want to pursue in the next year, identified on page 111. Add them to the first column of the chart on the following page. In the middle column, outline any support you might need to see this wish through, whether it's a person (like a therapist or an accountability partner); an emotion or quality (like grit or confidence); or even a tangible good, service, or product (like a writing class or equipment). It might also be something intangible (like time, effort, or money). In the last column, jot down what feels like a reasonable timeline for achieving this goal.

TOP FIVE WISHES TO PURSUE THIS YEAR	SUPPORT NEEDED	ETA
1.		
2.		
3.		
4.		
5.		

What are three small changes you can make TODAY in support of your goals?

It can be exciting but daunting to see your action plan on paper. But a series of small steps can lead to big results. Write down three small steps or changes you can make today in the boxes below. Make these changes as small as needed to accomplish them today. (For example, if you have a long-term health goal on your list, perhaps today's small change can be trying a five-minute yoga video at home or making an appointment with a new doctor.)

THREE SMALL CHANGES

1

2

3

What are three big changes you can make this year?

THREE BIG CHANGES

1

2

3

What additional support do you need to make these changes?

List them out. Think about the people, places, things, skills, and experiences that might be useful to you on your journey. Consider how the support you need may vary for big versus small changes.

BIG SUPPORT

_____

_____

_____

_____

_____

_____

_____

SMALL
SUPPORT

_____

_____

_____

_____

_____

_____

_____

WHO DO I WANT IN MY CORNER?

Who can keep you accountable? Be a cheerleader?
These may be people who help you stay focused when you get off track, boost your spirits when things get tough, give you tough love when it's needed, or provide advice, mentorship, or other guidance on your journey. Add names to your accountability circle here.

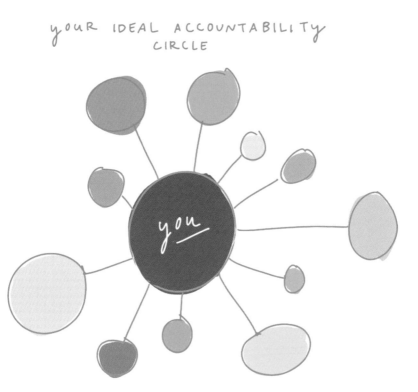

YOUR IDEAL ACCOUNTABILITY CIRCLE

you

Who can you reach out to TODAY for support?
What will you ask them for (support, advice, cheerleading, etc.)?
Name one person and what you will ask of them below.

WHO I'LL ASK

WHAT I'LL ASK THEM FOR

As you begin on your journey toward leading the life you want, take a moment to write a few words about how you are feeling right now.

It's time to make changes and architect the life you want. You have the clarity of what you seek, the heart behind your passions, and the guts to get things going. You know things might be hard, but if not now, when?

Now give yourself a pep talk.

What words do you need to hear from yourself to get started?
Let these words be a salve or a motivator for when the going
gets tough or even a celebration of what you've accomplished.
Return to these pages when you want a reminder of what
you've set out to pursue and why it matters.

I AM the ARCHITECT OF MY OWN LIFE

I AM

AM

MAKING

CHANGES

Notes

Use this space for capturing additional notes, impressions, and observations from your life audit or drilling down and expanding on any of your previous entries. You might also find it useful to brainstorm next steps, jot down notes from conversations with mentors, or summarize your personal insights and findings here.

NOTES

NOTES

NOTES

NOTES

NOTES

NOTES

NOTES

NOTES

NOTES

NOTES

NOTES

Acknowledgments

My gratitude goes to everyone who read my original blog post on the life audit and inspired me to make it something bigger. Thank you also to the many life auditors who tested new prompts and helped me refine old ones.

Special thanks also to my agent, Leila Campoli; my editor, Rachel Hiles; my design counterpart, Wynne Au-Yeung; and everyone at Chronicle who had a hand in making this book come true.

Much love to my family, who have been there for me since the beginning. To Isaac and Elio, you are always in my audit.

About the Author

Ximena Vengoechea is a user researcher, writer, and illustrator, and the creator of the life audit. She is the author of several nonfiction books and journals, including *Rest Easy: Discover Calm and Abundance through the Radical Power of Rest*, which received a starred review from *Library Journal* and was named one of Book Riot's Best Books of 2023; *Listen Like You Mean It: Reclaiming the Lost Art of True Connection*; and *The Life Audit: A Step-by-Step Guide to Discovering Your Goals and Building the Life You Want*. Her writing has appeared in *Inc.*, the *Washington Post*, *Newsweek*, *Forbes*, and *Fast Company*, among others. A user researcher by training, she has worked at Pinterest, LinkedIn, and Twitter. She lives in Brooklyn.

To learn more, visit ximenavengoechea.com, or sign up for her newsletter at ximena.substack.com. Vengoechea is available for select speaking engagements. To inquire about a possible appearance, visit ximenavengoechea.com/speaking.